Let the poor say I am

RICH

Poor

WestBow Press books may be ordered through booksellers or by contacting:

WestBow Press
A Division of Thomas Nelson & Zondervan
1663 Liberty Drive
Bloomington, IN 47403
www.westbowpress.com
844-714-3454

KJV - King James Version
Scripture taken from the King James Version of the Bible.

NIV – New International Version
Scriptures taken from the Holy Bible, New International Version®, NIV®. Copyright © 1973, 1978, 1984, 2011 by Biblica, Inc.™ Used by permission of Zondervan. All rights reserved worldwide. www.zondervan.com The "NIV" and "New International Version" are trademarks registered in the United States Patent and Trademark Office by Biblica, Inc.™ All rights reserved.

ISBN: 979-8-3850-3526-7 (sc)
ISBN: 979-8-3850-3527-4 (hc)
ISBN: 979-8-3850-3528-1 (e)

Library of Congress Control Number: 2024920937

Print information available on the last page.

WestBow Press rev. date: 10/02/2024

WESTBOW
PRESS®
A DIVISION OF THOMAS NELSON
& ZONDERVAN

Contents

POOR

The word above scares most of us. We try to fight against it, run or even out run poverty. We compare our own lifestyles to others, and then evaluate. Children know how to do this at a very young age. At some point there are many who begin to oppress those they deem to have less.

Chapter 1

- I came from a family of 5 children and our mom, was divorced. Many perceived us as poor. I never felt poor or thought about being poor. Until someone at school 5th grade describe me as poor. I had never thought about it. I woke up after this and realized more how we can be influenced by others' opinions of us. Oppression! I appreciate the use of the: just be kind signs, is that happening. It is a fruit of the Spirit. Kindness shows in what we do or fail to do. Our actions and what we say can be used to show kindness. Children use our actions to determine who is and who is not that important to us. I've experienced what people sometimes think about the poor. For many it doesn't feel kind or good.

GOD LOVES ALL OF US, RICH OR POOR. HE SAYS REMEMBER THE POOR. HE WANTS US ALL TO BE KIND.

Colossians 3:12 NIV

Therefore, as God's chosen people, holy and dearly loved, clothe yourselves with compassion, kindness, humility, gentleness and patience.

I wanted to include this scripture from the Bible, the Message version says:

"Master, please, I don't talk well. I've never been good with words, neither before nor after you spoke to me. I stutter and stammer". God responds, "And who do you think made the human mouth? And who makes some mute, some deaf, some sighted, some blind? Isn't it I, God? So, get going. I'll be right there with you- with your mouth! I'll be right there to teach you what to say". Exodus 4:10-12 MESSAGE

Today there is more help available to those in need. When we grew up, there was very little and most just learned to do without. I never really felt poor. Many people around me lived the same way we did. Most people worked hard and always had a garden. Beans and cornbread make for a real good meal, I love them. I also loved fried potatoes and onion. Tea and Coffee.

We do need to be kind. God's word tells parents to teach their children. Children pay attention and learn from what we do and say, our actions teach children. What we teach through His word and our actions are very important.

Kindness follows us. Kindness is a fruit of God's Spirit.

I, like the kind word, it's one used in the Bible, along with truth and honesty. The Bible's definition of kind, do unto others as you would have them do unto you and your family. We can't just do or say, or not say, whatever we want or what makes us comfortable with a smile and call that kind. Smiles don't necessary mean kind. It's kind when we hold God and others in higher esteem than ourself. We all need to practice these things.

Movies teach us there are fake personalities. Tears can be fake, love can be fake, and kindness can be fake. God can help us to have pure hearts.

Our words, our actions, the difference in how we treat people that are rich compared to poor. Children learn quick and they notice and they copy their parents and others they look up to.

Poor kids don't go on vacations and many don't wear clothes with labels that let the world believe they're rich. There are times when people might pass some down or they get them from a thrift store, yard sale or secondhand store. Bible says people love the rich and the poor are hated. The Bible also says, they are shunned, overlooked or ignored. Everyone wants to be one who is loved and accepted or looked up to.

We all like to have friends and feel accepted, no one enjoys being lonesome or hated.

In many ways it seems our nation and our families have almost forgot God. Our Father, He didn't abandon us. He loves us and still gives us our daily bread. I pray that the Lord helps us to turn our hearts towards Him. That we seek Him and ask for the things we need. He says ask. You do not have, because you do not ask. Ask and you shall receive.

Listen God is great. I know it's tough and we sweat when funds are low. By God's grace and love He sends provision, seems like it gets worse before it's better. When it does come, it's like a fresh rain. You look up and it seems like you can see His smiling face. We know He is good. He takes care of us. He likes a sacrifice of praise just remember to thank Him. Just sing Him a song.

There have been times that I just thought, there's no way for me to make it this month and somehow, I would. It's hard paying for the place you live, car payments, food, gas, utilities etc. it goes on and on.

There are those times when things run smooth and it's like a cherry on your ice cream/ dream almost for some of us. It's God, He kisses us and puts the smile on our face. It's the ups and downs that help grow us. Enabling us to be of help to our families and others. He comforts us so we can comfort others, with the same comfort. Good God He Is. You are loved.

7

God and the fruit of His Spirit can change all of us. When we say yes to God, He has the power to transform us.

We also need to be careful what our children or younger people hear coming out of months about others. Children especially pay attention when you talk about people in your family sisters and aunts, brothers and uncles. Your words effect how your children treat others and even who they love or don't love. Children are greatly influenced by their mothers and fathers. But we, will stand alone before the Lord. WE ALL KNOW THERES SUCH A BLESSING IN GRACE, THROUGH CHRIST. Children even know who's rich in the family and who's poor. Try not to make a difference. God knows all that goes on. He cares for the poor, even though the Bible says they are shunned and hated. Children get bullied in school because they are poor.

A person in Christ is deeper than that, we're pretty deep. All of us need to remember to treat others how we and our family wants to be treated. This is the instruction the Lord gave each of us. Loving one another.

Wealth makes many "friends"; poverty drives them all away.
Proverbs 19:4 NLT

Wealth makes many friends, But the poor is separated from his friend.
Proverbs 19:4 NKJV

I indeed have passion for the poor. I believe I was called and that we all are called. God has equipped and qualified us for the calling. O how I love JESUS, because He first loved me! Helping those that have less, is what I was created to do! Sometimes it has been really hard, all I can do is call out to Him and ask Him to supply the strength and the ability to continue on. I find rest and trust and before long, I am ready to go again.

We should all feel closer to the Lord when we are serving those who have less. I have been poor; some would say still poor. When He gives you a passion for a certain people, and an unexplainable love for them, and tops all that off with Joy, I think you're pretty much were he wants you. When your busy serving others, you're looking more like Him, He was a servant.

When we don't feel well or are having a bad day it is harder to practice kindness, it is however, again: fruit of His Spirit

Sometimes we just treat people how we think they treat us.

We need to try to remember what it is to love others as ourselves.

We need to ask the Father to help us to bring glory and praise to Him, and at the same time getting better at LOVE is always good. I love the hymn: Purer in Heart Help Me to Be.

God can and does use all of us. Rich or poor were needed in His World. We all have a Purpose.

Mom and 4 of us kids were returning from the grocery store, we passed a homeless man, just before we pulled in our drive. He was hungry we asked Mom if we could fix him a sandwich, she said yes. We're so excited to have his company, we fed him a good meal and visited with him a long time. We didn't want him to leave. We all noticed the top of his shoes were cut off, we asked him about it. He had cut them to make room for his toes.

We were taught to care for others and to always share what we had.

I didn't think we were poor, *because I wasn't taught that*. God, gave us food and home to live in, my mom had a good job. There wasn't a lot of financial aid then.

I didn't see us as poor. But according to this world and the young man, I mentioned above we were poor and so looked down upon. This is not kind. Again, I hope those just be kind signs are helping.

It's not so much the word poor that hurts, it's how the Bible says the poor are treated. Many do mistreat people they deem poor.

Should having a lot of money determine your value in the World? Children are comparing their family wealth to another child's family wealth. Kinda sick and isn't kind. Wealth is a blessing. However, God blesses all of us. We all contribute in the areas we are called.

God puts poor people on their feet again; he rekindles burned-out lives with fresh hope, restoring dignity and respect to their lives – a place in the sun! 1 Samuel 2:8 Message

"God is our refuge and strength, an ever-present help in trouble." Psalm 46:1 NIV

Embrace who you are in Christ Jesus, He made you! Let yourself, your home, you be different than everyone else.

Step out of the race and competition. Breath in God, receive His peace and contentment. Focus on God and finishing the race Apostle Paul speaks about.

I know what it is to be in need, and I know what it is to have plenty. I have learned the secret of being content in any and every situation, whether well fed or hungry, whether living in plenty or in want. I can do all this through him who gives me strength.
Philippians 4:12-13 NIV

Spur one another on toward love and good deeds.
Hebrews 10:24-25 NIV

Be faithful in our little practices of love which make us more Christlike.

When our bills are paid, and we have something to eat, give at Church and feed someone we don't know how would I think I was poor? People who try to make someone look bad or less because of financial status in front of others, to feel good or better about themselves. This goes on in the world, in families, everywhere.

Some only what to be in the company of their rich friends and relatives. Forgetting it is God who cares for us and meets our needs.

Think about it. We indeed needed/need Jesus and forgiveness.

When you go to somebody's home, that's their home, they can't wait to get there from school or work or even vacation. They live there (HOME), it may not look as nice as yours, but they live there. Don't insult them, by saying why do you live here. They worked all week, really hard, just so they could live there, this is home. They might worship the Lord there maybe more than at Church. Church is once or twice a week. They live in their home every day. They worship God daily. Hold one another in higher regard than self.

"Do nothing out of selfish ambition or vain conceit, but in
humility consider others better than yourselves."
Philippians 2:3 NIV

I see this comparing in my own family, comparing our wealth to someone else to determine a person's own value. Type of car, type of house, which side of town you live on. Brand of clothes or shoes. Where you vacationed. Is this really kind? We sometimes even know another's wealth by where they go to church.

The Bible says: Chose today who you will serve, God or money. God knows we all need money. God blesses us with money and jobs and education. It's a blessing. He blesses us so we can bless others.

He that trusteth in his riches shall fall; but the righteous shall flourish as a branch. Proverbs 11:28 KJV

Do we have to be so competitive. Maybe we all need to cloth ourselves with compassion. Read Colossians 3:12 NIV

Keep your mind on things above, be a servant, do good deeds. Talking to our families, friends and neighbors, or visiting them. Especially the elderly. They are so beautiful when their faces light up at the sight of you.

The reason for telling this story is I Love that my mom taught us children about God. We learned: let the poor say I am rich.

There are poor people the Bible tells us there always will be poor people.

Jesus replied, Foxes have dens and birds have nest, but the Son of Man has no place to lay his head. – Matthew 8:20 NIV

When He gives you a passion for a certain people, and an unexplainable love for them, and tops all that off with joy, I think you're pretty much, where He wants you. I love the poor, broken, and the downtrodden.

The poor are people. I in many ways since I was a child, have been there. I believe, this is the meaning: to be a follower of Christ – sacrifice. I want to be Spiritually filled every day of my life. I want to work hard and be used by Him. I want to be next to our Lord, he's serving somewhere. He gives us the love we give out to others. It flows through Him to His creation.

Just A Closer Walk, With Thee, Is My Plea.

When I see the Lord work in my life and also the others' he has allowed me to meet It takes my breath away. – He is so powerful and loving to all of us! He is who He says He is.

Sometimes the person you think is poor doesn't even realize they are poor cause they are busy loving Jesus and others. It's exciting! Let the poor say I am rich.

I had to by faith in Him step out into the field, I do mean field. Be willing to work, cooking, washing dishes, praying, crying, accepting all the insults, persecution (it happens). But then THERE IS JESUS...WHAT A SAVIOR OF US ALL! AND THERE WAS LOVE, LIKE I NEVER KNEW...OH SO BEAUTIFUL!

FOR MANY ARE CALLED, BUT FEW ARE CHOSEN. Matthew 22:14 KJV

WE LOVE BECAUSE HE FIRST LOVED US. 1 John 4:19 NIV

We learn that He would do immeasurably more than we could ask for or imagine. THIS IS SO TRUE! Ephesians 3:20 NIV

Have you notice Job, he was rich. In the Book of Job, we learn he was respected by young and old men for remembering the poor. Poor are not always homeless. Poor mother with children or poor father with children, or the elderly, anyone could be poor.

The word poor means a lot of things, not just financial.

We need to just tap into the Lord's Love more towards Him and each other. Love and compassion, clothe ourselves in it.

After I graduated, I worked for a wealthy family, learned so much from them. They owned all kinds of businesses around Indianapolis. They occasionally worked homeless men. I would pick homeless men up downtown Indy, daily. I would cook for them breakfast or lunch that day. Got to know them. I learned I loved the poor; they were interesting and usually kind. I worked for this family many years and also became like family to them.

I hold the poor or any one, who is in need close to my heart and in my prayers. The truth is we all need others and we can grow relationships through offering a hand to someone Poor or Rich. Life is hard for all people at times.

To feel oppressed is not a good feeling. The Bible talks about oppression a lot and the poor a lot. The poor are among us.

> "Real encouragement occurs when words are spoken from
> a heart of love to another's fear." Larry Crabb.
> Sometimes words cannot express so we need to listen to their heart.

Judging others because they have less income. O' you might say: We don't judge. Maybe we all might need to think about that. Do we behave as some people are not as important to us. Who are you spending most of your time with. An old saying was: it's who you know.

Bible says we shun the poor, and give presents to the rich.

Rich the Bible says pretends to be poor and the poor pretend to be rich. Bible says rich have more friends. It also warns about too many friends. There is one who sticks closer than a brother.

Truth is only God knows who's really rich and who's poor. He measures differently.

29 All the rich of the earth will feast and worship; all who go down to the dust will kneel before him – those who cannot keep themselves alive. 30 Posterity will serve him; future generations will be told about the Lord. 31 They will proclaim his righteousness, declaring to a people yet unborn: He has done it!
Psalm 22:29-31 NIV

4 For you make me glad by your deeds, LORD; I sing for joy at what your hands have done. 5 How great are your works, LORD, how profound your thoughts!
Psalm 92:4-5 NIV

Chapter 2

My husband and I reach out to the homeless (some homeless are not poor and not everyone who is poor is homeless). We also work with people who struggle with addiction or other problems. We felt a desire to do this and with very little we stepped out, including experience. We just started cooking and feeding and studying the Bible around firepits in homeless camps. Also cooked twice a week downtown for a Bible Study. Used vegetables from our garden. Even took turnip greens and cornbread, they loved it! One 18 yr. old ate 3 plates full of collard greens and cornbread.

One time when we were out there were 78 people in line behind my car and I thought for sure I was going to run out of food before the day was over, we had several more stops. We didn't run out of food. I never have. Reminded me of the food and what was left over when Jesus fed the 5,000, folks it is still Jesus feeding all of us. With God all things are possible. I love it. Thank You Lord, for teaching me and showing me WHO YOU ARE!

Beautiful... Jesus came in like a STORM, He filled me up! The gospel was in plain view for me now. Takes my breath away even now, as I type. Bible says filled with Joy and the Spirit! No one has to tell me Who's rich or poor. We're all BLESSED.

After seeing and learning some of things the Lord has taught. I think I might sing louder than any other person at Church.

"Shout with joy to the LORD, all the earth! Psalm 100:1 NIV

"Let the whole world glorify the Lord; let it sing his praise." Isaiah 42:12 NLT

("Who is like you O Lord?) With your unfailing love you lead the people you have redeemed. In your might, you guide them to your sacred home." Exodus 15:13 NLT

Tell you, I get so excited.

May the glory of the Lord continue forever! The Lord takes pleasure in all he has made. Psalm 104:31 NLT

I know one thing I believe I benefited more, than anybody I thought I was serving. The hard work God made easy. The food and the expense seemed to work out because of GOD! Some in the beginning started wanting to help us. The Church would give us leftovers. God just moved in. I get so excited. I love when I see God at work and sense His leading and presence.

The Lord was really teaching me about trusting and faith, and love how beautiful it is. God is so good! I love all of it. I was in His class room, still am, in His class room and I'm getting old. I now have begun to forget things. Wow, that's wild. I have always been known for having a memory, it's going.

I give you thanks, O LORD, with all my heart; I will sing your praises...

Psalm 138:1 NLT

Thou hast been a shelter for me.

3 For You have been a shelter for me. A strong tower from the enemy.

4 I will abide in Your tabernacle forever; I will trust in the shelter of Your wings.

Psalm 61:3 – 4 NKJV

The generous will themselves be blessed, for they share their food with the poor.

Proverbs 22:9 NIV

And

13 The LORD stands up to plead, And stands to judge the people.

14 The LORD will enter into judgement With the elders of His people and His princes:

"For you have eaten up the vineyard; The plunder of the poor is in your houses.

15 "What do you mean by crushing My people and grinding the face of the poor? Says the Lord God of hosts.

Isaiah 3:13-15 NKJV

Mary, the mother of Jesus, is described as a servant girl.

Jesus, was always looking for servants. Jesus came to serve and not be served. We are to serve others to bring life and light to what was dead.

A life of sacrifice says pick up your cross. Step in to the troubles around you be a light. Give the hope you have in Jesus. There are messes and there is brokenness and darkness in our families and on the street. We need to make the choice, to step in and help. Love looks like sacrifice/service.

1 Timothy 6:17-19 NIV

Command those who are rich in this present world not to be arrogant nor to put their hope in wealth, which is so uncertain, but to put their hope in God, who richly provides us with everything for our enjoyment.

By his divine power, God has given us everything we need for living a Godly life. We have received all of this by coming to know him, the one who called us to himself by means of his marvelous glory and excellence. 2 Peter 1:3 NLT

It takes all of us together, we each one are made in His image, looking at each other we get a clearer picture of Him. One alone can't contain WHO HE IS. It takes us all imitating Him in our life of service prompted by love.

As I mentioned before we got insulted, persecuted by many people. Family, friends, some at Church and others. That all hurt, but hey maybe we learned a thing or two. Apostle Paul, said Christ, he was preached! (Philippians 1)

Father, when You show Yourself, Your love, we gain courage and strength, You're Awesome God.

Chapter 3

I mentioned earlier, we also work with people who struggle with addiction. We met some sweet families, from church. Someone sitting next to you, could be struggling. The person sitting behind you at church might be the neediest person you meet that day. Church is a hospital for the soul. Many people go when they are hurting. Looking for comfort.

God works powerfully in all our lives. He works on all of us. He's at the wheel, the (Potter continues to form the clay).

Apostle Paul said he was chief of all sinners. We may be able to join him. Bible says: No, not one, all fall short.

Don't put others down, unless it's on your prayer list. The Bible never mentions warning about Dishonoring the Rich only the Poor. The poor do get oppressed. In the book of James, the Church was warned about dishonoring the poor. We have to be careful in how we treat people who have less than us. Look you'll see how many ways they are richer in Christ, in life, in love, I'm talking Bible not world. We all at times get in the trap of the world.

One Wednesday afternoon, I was getting the food ready for the Bible Study and Lunch.

When a young man (David) came in, he had been verbally attacked, as he was walking in the snow to Bible Study, long cold walk. He had never believed in God and now was a lover of Jesus. He grew up in a Foster Home and now was on the streets. HE WAS 6'4" CAME TO ME CRYING, he needed someone to give him comfort. Because, he stopped to get coffee and people cursed him said he was dirty no good homeless and lazy. People do say that. There were several young people who grew up in Foster Care. They now live on the street.

I remember several who were in college, downtown Indianapolis, living on the street. There was a School Teacher, his wife passed away, he went through depression/mental illness, he is now returned to teaching.

Not everyone who is poor, are homeless. Some families struggle paying monthly debts and then needing food and clothing, etc.

ITS NOT JUST THE HOMELESS THAT STRUGGLE WITH BEING POOR. ANYONE CAN BE POOR.

I am blessed because I've turned into an old mother hen. I love all of them so much. I love in the book Colossians, especially 3:12 NLT.

12 Since God chose you to be the holy people he loves, you must clothe yourselves with tenderhearted mercy (compassion), kindness, humility, gentleness, and patience.

You called out to GOD. ... He put your feet on a wonderful road that took you straight to a good place to live. So, thank GOD for his marvelous love, for his miracle mercy to the children he loves. He poured great draughts of water down parched throats; the starved and hungry got plenty to eat. – Psalm 107:6-9 MESSAGE

All of your works will thank you, Lord, and your faithful followers will praise you. They will speak of the glory of your kingdom; they will give examples of your power. They will tell, about your mighty deeds and about the majesty and glory of your reign. For your kingdom is an everlasting kingdom. You rule throughout all generations. – Psalm 145:10-13 NLT

"Let the whole world glorify the Lord; let it sing his praise." -Isaiah 42:12 NLT

I love to sing!

O' you would have melted if you heard this beautiful voice that broke out after lunch one Friday, at the Bible Study lunch. She was homeless was passing through Indianapolis, she heard about the Bible Study and lunch and she blessed God and us with her beautiful voice as she sang to Him, hymns. She enjoyed her lunch and drank a lot of sweet tea.

When I see what God does, it captures me. Beautiful beyond description!

There were times I just wanted to stay in the moment. I don't remember ever feeling so connected to our LORD.

I had read, study, went to church and needed all of it and loved it. This was something different for me. I was at His feet. He had my attention. I was growing and learning and relearning. Refreshed and loving like I never had. I had loved and served the homeless since I was 21 but this was different, my husband and I had invested more and we received more from it. Have I told you lately: JESUS HE IS BEAUTIFUL!

29

5 But if anyone obeys his word, love for God is truly made complete in them. This is how we know we are in him: 6 Whoever claims to live in him must live as Jesus did. – 1 John 2:5-6 NIV

Having "the aroma of Christ"

14 But thanks be to God, who always leads us as captives in Christ's triumphal procession and uses us to spread the aroma of the knowledge of him everywhere. 15 For we are to God the pleasing aroma of Christ among those who are being saved and those who are perishing. 16 To the one we are an aroma that brings death; to the other, an aroma that brings life. And who is equal to such a task? 17 unlike so many, we do not peddle the word of God for profit.

On the contrary, in Christ we speak before God with sincerity, as those sent from God. 2 Corinthians 2:14-17 NIV

My Mother, would go with me to take lunch and stay for Bible Study, my mom loved it. They became like family to us. Once when I was going to their camps along the river, my mom was with me. She began to feel bad, her sugar had dropped we were in the woods, down a long trail, one of the homeless gave her a drink from a pop he was drinking and she drank it.

My Mom, wasn't worried about germs, she just drank it. I love my mom, she passed away, 6 years ago. She had dementia. She never forgot us or God. She, taught me so much, she was a servant. Once, years before this time, someone needed shoes, she took hers off and went barefoot, she gave her shoes away. Now you tell me who's poor.

Rich in Love! (Math – Mom taught me, she learned it from

the Bible). I miss my Mom, her company, she was my friend. Jesus, taught all of us that math. Faith to trust Him more.

Some examples of Jesus math:153 Fish, 2 fish/5 loaves and also a few fish/7 loaves. Don't forget what was left over after he had fed everyone. He provided our food in the beginning in the Garden of Eden. There were animals and vegetation. He provides. Water turned to wine for a wedding. He told Peter some money they needed was in a fish's mouth. I love these fish stories, they are true.

Peter went and got it. He had taken care of us, before He even put us here. WHAT A "SAVIOR"

"You have enough you need only to share it." faith/trust If you give me your little, I will break it up for you and let you give it to others. Then I'll return it to you increased a hundredfold. Jesus and his math, I learned this as a poor child, it is true. God does bless us when we are obedient to his word.

When I am broken Christ can shine through me. We do have tribulation and we do hurt and suffer. Christ uses this in preparing us for the work he has decided for us to do.

Heavenly Father, help us to see others' needs, to hear their cries and respond with love and compassion.

Bind us together, Lord, with cords that cannot be broken.

Bind us together with love.

In Jesus Sweet Name Amen

The Lord cares for all of us and he feeds us physically and spiritually. He puts the right people, at the right time, those he has prepared to help us. He is at work in each person's life the caregiver and the receiver. We are His clay.

We all have value he paid a high price for each of us.

This is only a portion of His love.

You know our King was born in a manger. As He grew, He began to teach us. Many marveled at His wisdom. He told us He had no place to lay His head. He rode a borrowed donkey. He was mocked and looked down on. He had only a few friends. He served food and washed feet. He touched people who were sick and got them on their feet. He raised the dead. He wept. He fed thousands, fish and bread. He never looked down on others until He died to pay their debt. He prayed for all of us before He hung His head.

Jesus, knows what it is like to live poor, He felt it.

If you don't know Him, I pray you learn to know Him. He is comfort because He knows what it is to hurt and feel so alone.

I know how often I have turned to him and found comfort. Sometimes when we have needs, we have to wait. I have found when He does come to me it's refreshing like a drink of water that goes down easy, it is relief. Relief that brings the most comfort, nothing else as unique. Yes, He's felt it.

Chapter 4

Israel is in our prayers.

Israel's leaders took charge, and the people gladly followed. Praise the LORD! Listen, you Kings! Pay attention, you mighty rulers! For I will sing to the LORD. I will make music to the LORD the God of Israel. – Judges 5:2-3 NLT

God, is near to all created.

The family I am working for tomorrow, he is Jewish. I have worked for them close to 20 years. I love them. She is such a loving and caring person. She was telling me all about Israel. I have never been there. I take her vegetables from my garden and fresh eggs and flower seeds. Her and I would laugh and say, and jelly. I love to make jelly. She loves the strawberry. We have grown older together. They have been good to us. I am a Gar.den.er, (who loves gardening), very hard work. I Love it!

I, just came in my husband and I, have been digging our sweet potatoes. So much fun, my favorite to harvest! It's like an Easter egg hunt.

When the movie FAITH LIKE POTATOS came out, MY FRIENDS ALL CALLED. THEY KNEW I WOULD LOVE THAT MOVIE...AND I DID!

I love potatoes. One Potato – Two Potatoes.

I have been so blessed!

Remember Naomi and Ruth poor widows.

Remember the widow Elijah went to? She gave from her little and then had plenty of flour and oil.

Lazarus and the rich man.

It is so easy for any of us to fall into greed. Our hearts need to be soft. Apostle Paul said he had learned to be content. Seems we're always rushing around wanting or coveting and more and more.

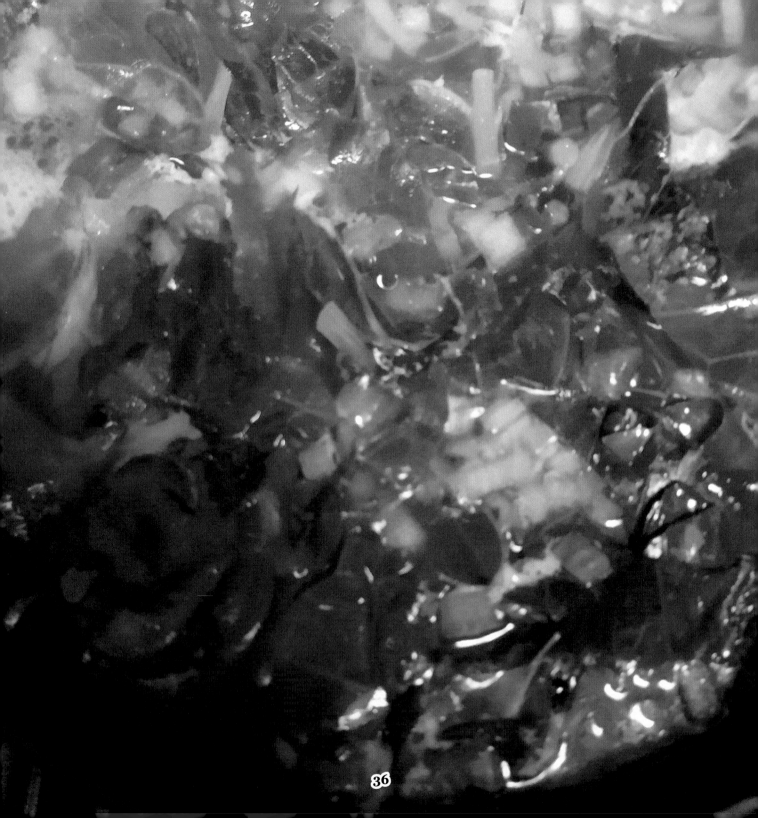

A generous man will himself be blessed, for he shares his bread with the poor.

Proverbs 22:9 Berean Standard Bible

We earn a check, but it's what we give that makes us rich.

I give you thanks, O LORD, with all my heart; I will sing your praises...

Psalm 138:1 NLT

It is about the fruit of the Spirit: 22 But the fruit of the Spirit is Love, Joy, Peace, Forbearance, Kindness, Goodness, Faithfulness, 23 Gentleness and Self-Control; against such things there is no law. -Galatians 5:22-23 NIV

The worlds thinking sometimes sounds similar to God's. Most times it's not. God's word is WISDOM and TRUTH, and comes from perfect LOVE. Often, I have to examine what I am hearing and pray and get into God's word. Just take another look at Jesus and His example.

Most of what we have is material stuff and loses its value almost immediately. True riches or "Great Wealth" is found only in Christ. He said let the poor say I am rich. We're rich.

19 "Do not store up for yourselves treasures on earth, where moths and vermin destroy, and where thieves break in and steal. 20 But store up for yourselves treasures in heaven, where moths and vermin do not destroy. And where thieves do not break in and steal. 21 For where your treasure is, there your heart will be also.

Matthew 6:19-21 NIV

Psalm 89:52 NIV

Praise be to the LORD forever! Amen and Amen

EMMANUEL

Jesus, (came down) from Heaven for you and me. He lived among us. He sat and talked and He stayed for a visit. He taught us, He healed us, and took time to listen. He was God with us, Emmanuel!

Jesus, freed us from poverty, abuse and disease. He opened our eyes, then we could see, and our ears we began to hear.

Jesus gave us bread and the fruit of the vine we drink, we do this, in remembrance of Him. You see, He knew there was a tree. He taught us baptism, after this clothed us in a robe, and breathed a new life in us, Him.

Jesus, Thank You for your pleas at Gethsemane, the blood, the sweat, the tears and Your life that you gave for me.

You are the Alpha and the Omega, the beginning and the end. From the Old to the New and before Abraham and his many seed, you said: **I** AM. You already knew Abraham and his many, many, seeds. You are the one who hung on the tree. You are part of the Trinity. You knew from the beginning in the garden there would be the tree at Calvary.

You are beautiful beyond description, you thought of all the SEED.

I can witness, I know what You've done in and for me. Lord, you saved a wretch, when You saved me.

I pray others see and believe!

ksuhls

Jesus, we Thank You! Jesus, we Thank You and We Thank You, for setting us free!

When we began to feed those that were in need, I carried this scripture in my heart:

12 And He also went on to say to the one who had invited Him, "When you give a luncheon or a dinner, do not invite your friends or your brothers or your relatives or rich neighbors, otherwise they may also invite you in return and that will be your repayment. 13 "But when you give a reception, invite the poor, the crippled, the lame, the blind, 14 and you will be blessed, since they do not have the means to repay you; for you will be repaid.

Luke 14:12-14 NIV

Jesus cared deeply about the poor and the downtrodden. The poor in their helplessness, put their trust in God.

I've heard said there are over 2,000 Bible verses about remembering to poor.

Jesus knew what it was to be poor, forsaken by friends and left alone, to be thirsty and weary, to have enemies revile him, to have sleepless nights wrestling in prayer for those who didn't appreciate him, to suffer pain and the Cross, crying out to God the Father. He had no friends he was insulted, hated Crucified.

Have you ever felt any of the above, it's tuff stuff.
Matthew 21:14 NIV

The blind and the lame came to him in at the temple, and he healed them. He had compassion.

Sweet Jesus.

A man who had no place to lay his head.

13 The LORD standeth up to plead, and standeth to judge the people. 14 The LORD will enter into judgment with the ancients of his people, and the princes thereof: for ye have eaten up the vineyard; the spoil of the poor is in your houses. 15 What mean ye that ye beat my people to pieces, and grind the faces of the poor? Saith the Lord GOD of hosts.

Isaiah 3:13-15 KJV

Proverbs 23

20 Do not be with heavy drinkers of wine, or with gluttonous eaters of meat; 21 For the heavy drinker and the glutton will come to poverty, and drowsiness will clothe one with rags.

Proverbs 23:20-21 NASB

Proverbs 20:1 ESV Wine is a mocker, strong drink a brawler, and whoever is intoxicated by it is not wise.

My husband shared this scripture with one man downtown and he said, I don't like Proverbs. He had been drinking a lot that day and was wanting to fight.

I READ this one day it said: Rich in kindness, generosity and thankfulness. I want to be that way.

Apostle Paul was told to remember the poor, the very thing he was eager to do.

One Christmas, was very hard on my husband and I. We didn't think I would feel like going out, I had been in the hospital. I wanted to go. It was Christmas Eve. We did make it out. The last homeless person we came to: she was a young gal with down syndrome, face was like an angel, I loved her and I needed her. We had taken presents to each one of the homeless, something just for each of them.

We only had a few things left, but enough for her we told her to pick out what she wanted, overjoyed it was so cute, we gave all that was left to her. I'm telling you God is Good! What a blessing. We never seen her again, but will never forget her. She was an angel.

Don't ever believe a poor person has nothing to offer, they do. She made our Christmas. She showed more joy and love than any child I have ever seen. It didn't take much. Her sweetness was a gift to me.

Not everyone who is poor is lazy, a drunk, or mentally ill, some are; however, they are still people and still have souls. Made in His Image. Most are working, sleeping, and paying their bills. Like others.

Lots of people drink and get drunk, lots of people have had mental breakdowns, and some get by being lazy. Not just the homeless, as many believe.

Poor people are not always homeless, we were poor and lived in a home. Sometimes they live in houses nicer than yours or homes old and ran down.

Sometimes people have been abused, struggle with life, they lose their jobs, they get too old to work. There might be a reason for their situation.

I am so grateful that people seem to be more compassionate for people with mental illness. Most, I think can relate to anguish, depression and anxiety. Life can be hard.

We live in a rented, 150 years old tiny farmhouse. Been here 20 years. I have had 4 different teenagers live with me over the years, at different times. I get put down for this old house why would I rent and not own a new house. I have worked, most of my life. I love living here. I've even helped many of those who put me down. That's ok I'll cry to Jesus. He'll say shake off the dust and put on a beautiful dress and remember you are loved. (They don't realize, it's all only rented).

I'm writing this because I do observe what goes on around me and I also listen. This nonsense is passing on to our children. They see you do nice things, especially at Christmas. Most people give gifts at Christmas. They are paying attention to you, yourself and I. Your conduct and what you are saying, maybe favoring those who have lots of riches/money. Children are listening and watching, not just yours. Even other peoples' children are watching you. There are some riches worth having. Sent from above. But some are just material. There is nothing wrong with enjoying nice things, but when you say hurtful things or place yourselves above others by words or action it's ugly and it hurts.

Remember the signs: Just be kind. (kindness fruit of the Spirit)

11 Come, my children, listen to me; I will teach you the fear of the LORD,

12 whoever of you loves life and desires to see many good days, 13 keep your tongue from evil and your lips from telling lies.
Psalm 34:11-13 NIV

My husband and I were invited to a child's Birthday party and everyone brought gifts one child brought a coloring book and crayons and child receiving the gift said, coloring book and crayons, is this all you brought me. She pushed it away. It starts young, that is why we are told to teach. To pass on the things of God. The people that brought the gift was affected. It hurt you can see hurt in a person face.

It's so easy to say the wrong things, we have all did it. We need to be reminded to be kind the Holy Spirit does correct us. Then we can begin to make necessary changes in our behavior and our thoughts –they have away usually to surface. Children copy us when they're young.

Children know who gives the most money and who's presents are of less value, and the ones that cost more. When focus, is more on love and service, life is richer. I've seen families where that was their focus and the children in that home grew to become great leaders. No matter where the road turned.

There is always more in God's word on any subject, seek His guidance.

Wherefore be ye not unwise, but understanding what the will of the Lord is. Ephesians 5:17 KJV

Not everybody that serves gets paid, Apostle Paul brought that subject up also. He didn't mind reminding those around him. He was insulted many times, under attacked, and in prisoned. He was called! Jesus, told us the cost, it's high. In this we're now discussing true riches. We cannot, serve both God and Money, he says. You will be insulted and persecuted by some and it hurts. Fix your heart and mind on Christ, he will strengthen you.

Sometimes we all need to examine ourself, this is important. Bible tells each of us this. We also need each other. In Proverbs it talks about the cord not easily broken.

Zechariah 7:9-10 NIV

9 "This is what the LORD almighty said: "Administer true justice; show mercy and compassion to one another. 10 Do not oppress the widow or the fatherless, the foreigner or the poor. Do not plot evil against each other."

I am around a lot of young families with children. Bible said pass on from one generation to the next. His love endures forever. I love that.

Proverbs 3 the entire chapter covers what I am writing. I feel sorrow from what I hear and see in the world today.

There is good and God is here. His spirit abides with us, in us.

I feel afraid and hurt over what seems to go unnoticed. We need to turn the man- made lights down with all the sparkle, and let His light shine forth even brighter.

Does any of us need to sparkle that much? We're all special God made us in His image.

Amen to that.

"Praise the LORD, O my soul. O LORD my God, you are very great; you are clothed with splendor and majesty". Ps 104:1 NIV

1 Give praise to the LORD, proclaim his name; make known among the nations what he has done.

2 Sing to him, sing praise to him; tell of all his wonderful acts.

3 Glory in his holy name; let the hearts of those who seek the LORD rejoice.

Ps. 105:1-3 NIV

Chapter 5

Many are looking at the outward appearance. You might appear Rich, we're to fix our eyes on Christ, the Bible says riches, fly away. Bible says they put riches in bags that have holes. Kindness is fruit of His Spirit.

Money is needed but God is needed MOST. Seek His Kingdom first.

I was a poor kid, but I knew inside I was RICH. Self-worth valued by God's definition not mans.

In Junior High School, I was shy, poor – remember, a popular boy, football player, his sister was a cheerleader. He thought he would spit on me, that was painful everyone seen him do it.

At times it was really hard to go to school. I'm old and this, it still hurts.

When you're poor, shy and not one of the popular ones, sometimes you are easy prey. Mostly because your counted as not. You wouldn't speak up, and so you get abused and mistreated.

Thinking about it reminds me; that the Lord told us, these same things happened to Him and they would happen to us. He was hated, spit on, shunned we will be too, even by our own families He said. He was and He said, we will.

Jesus and His disciples were hated. Jesus, was killed on a CROSS.

Disciples were jailed, beheaded, hung on a Cross and hated. Looked down upon. Many came to him in secret or at night, so not to be seen.

Jesus, life was not easy. He said don't worry if they hate you, they hated Him. JESUS CAME TO SERVE AND NOT BE SERVED.

The pious seemed to treat Him the worst.

Many of those who were following Him, deserted Him. He asked the others if they wanted to walk away too.

The Truth is we all have reason to bow our head from shame.

Love for all of us put Jesus on the CROSS. He was there for each of us.

He, is the reason for our Hope!

The Lord has met all our needs, Provided for us. He does this continually.

Pause right here. I need to.

It's painful to think what Jesus, went through, sweat blood, the anguish and He cried: MY GOD MY GOD WHY HAVE THOU FORSAKEN ME?

We have been SAVED! CHRIST DIED FOR US.

Think about the ways He blesses us each day.

He equips us to pass onto others a portion of those blessings. He uses us, we get to share in the work of His kingdom.

Our praises and thanksgiving are crowns at His feet. We honor Him in service and humility.

The joy of being near Him. To feel Him at your side. Life at its best is when we stay connected to Him.

Sometimes I get side tracked and I sense loneliness and realize I moved not Him and He draws me back.

If I notice I am depressed I begin to count my blessings and before long mercy drops round me are falling.

My garden is doing great. I have begun harvesting and putting food up. God provides.

He gives us extra so we can share.

I even enjoy the work, Happy is the person whos' work and pleasure are one.

Jesus prayed for us that we could be one as He and the Father were one. He sent us the helper, our counselor to help us and He teaches us. "Rabboni".

I encourage anyone to examine their own life and see how He has cared for them throughout their life. He is there when things are well and He carries us through the tough stuff. The Bible says how beautiful are the feet. They are. He teaches us and cares for us.

For God so loved the world that He gave His only begotten Son, that whosoever believeth in Him should not perish but have everlasting life. John 3:16 KJV

How beautiful upon the mountains are the feet of him that bringeth good tidings, that publisheth peace; that bringeth good tidings of good, that pulisheth salvation; that saith unto Zion, Thy God reigneth! Isaiah 52:7 KJV

54

Someone please, pass the mashed potatoes from the garden. Oh, they taste good, God sent them to me! I'm harvesting potatoes today, love it! Wish my mom was here to help me. In the simplest things, the poor can say I am rich. A taste of the Goodness of God. Some like a little pepper.

I love to make a great shout unto the LORD! Sometimes I do it right from the middle of my garden...GOD IS GOOD!

Gardening on my mind love these scriptures:

And the LORD shall guide thee continually and satisfy thy soul in drought, and make fat thy bones: and thou shalt be like a watered garden, and like a spring of water, whose waters fail not.

Isaiah 58:11 KJV

They that dwell under his shadow shall return; they shall revive as the corn, and grow as the vine: the scent thereof shall be as the wine of Lebanon. Hosea 14:7 KJV

"The grass withers and the flowers fall, but the word of God endures forever. Isaiah 40:8 NIV

It's beautiful how God uses what we know to teach us His ways. He is so loving, He is LOVE!

Again, with this scripture, it comforts us.

God puts poor people on their feet again; he rekindles burned-out lives with fresh hope, restoring dignity and respect to their lives – a place in the sun!

1 Samuel 2:8 Message

God loves us and He disciplines those He loves.

Once I started working, I thought I was it. I enjoyed working. I bought and still do the best I Could AFFORD. I have had my own business many years, not rich but I lived good. Sometimes running from here to there, everybody at church would say slow down Kim slow down. Age, has begun doing that for me. I do still have energy. Now I have a sweet husband I met him at church while we were there working. I lived single a long time. Worked all the time, people at church would tell me, you should be on payroll. We'd laughed, I loved being at church. Work is fun to me. Signing up for S.S. next month. Semi- retired.

I love God. My Husband loves God.
I've learned it's a little at a time and it takes a life time.
Remember that song Love Lifted Me. There - is where it's at. Love does lift us.
But none saith, where is God my maker, who giveth songs in the night;
Job 35:10 KJV

I just this morning finished reading the book of Colossians it is encouraging. God's word and our relationship with Him and others is valuable. Unity! Church (the body) sweet fellowship in the Lord.

Softly and Tenderly: He is calling today!

By his divine power, God has given us everything we need for living a godly life. We have received all of this by coming to know him, the one who called us to himself by means of his marvelous glory and excellence. And because of his glory and excellence, he has given us great and precious promises. These are the promises that enable you to share his divine nature and escape the world's corruption caused by human desires.

2 Peter 1:3-4 NLT

As I have been writing this, in my heart I have a young man on my mind, who is close to me. He has seen so many worldly riches, he craves them. I can't seem to get him to notice the true riches. He watches those he thinks are wealthy. He has a large family 4 young children. He is sweet, he needs time and a desire to come to Jesus. Hope he notices the richness there is in Christ. His family, four babies they would flourish in the light of Christ. I love him and pray daily for him. Jesus and God are the Gold at the end of the Rainbow. He has suffered a great lost and gone through deep depression.

He's just one, I see it often. It hurts, there are souls not just bellies that need fed.

Sometimes myself included we just want more so we are accepted. Sometimes when people think your poor or not as educated you couldn't possibly have something to say that was of any value. God has a way of gently correcting these attitudes, but in the mean time they hurt.

It's early in the morning. This is my time with God. I have felt the internal tears often this morning. I know the Lord and He is with us. He will enable us to serve Him today. This is Love to our Lord, to care about those He cares about. Let us pray. Lord, be with us and may those we serve, see YOU today. In Your Sweet Name. Amen.

JESUS LOVES US!

We will be going out to feed all our babies (animals), soon. I added two baby chickens to my coop, they are big enough, seems they adapted well. I love them. We have lots of animals. Farm life.

I do a lot of baking and the fresh eggs are wonderful. My husband takes care of the horses down the street at another farm.

I also need to work in my garden. Pull weeds and pick tomatoes and green beans.

Today I'm off so I get to work with my own flowers and landscape and garden. I am excited.

Yesterday I took green beans and tomatoes to a beautiful lady who works me. She also was excited. Everyone enjoys fresh produce and fresh eggs.

Today, I plan to stuff some hot peppers and slice some big ripe red tomatoes, I'll also fix mashed potatoes from the garden. Should be a good meal.

The deer always help themselves to the garden. They been eating my corn and also the ate 10 heads of cabbage. I have 4 cabbages left hope they save those for us.

I love to make kraut.

If you don't have a garden, you should try it. It's fun and you get exercise and grow beautiful flowers and vegetables.

Children always love it.

You can share it with family and friends. Even preserving/canning etc. is fun. Again, it is work. Rewarding.

It is so exciting to watch your seeds grow. I even enjoy the animals that eat my vegetables. I just plant enough for them and us.

We grow all kinds of fruit and I make homemade jelly and jam.

Luke 8:5 NIV "A farmer went out to sow his seed. As he was scattering the seed, some fell along the path; it was trampled on, and birds ate it up. 6 Some fell on rocky ground, and when it came up, the plants withered because they had no moisture. 7 Other seed fell among thorns, which grew up with it and choked the plants. 8 Still other seed fell on good soil. It came up and yielded a crop, a hundred times more than was sown." When he said this, he called out, "Whoever has ears to hear, let them hear."

We have helped in the past with gardens downtown Indianapolis. Gardening is part of my trade for many years. I love the garden.

Some of the people downtown have ducks and chickens too. I love all my sweet little feathered babies.

The following are some of the people we notice, who might need help:

Often a Single parent struggles, they do get some help. The elderly struggle with finances and most of all many are lonely and afraid. We all need someone to help at times. Don't forget the young people sometimes they need us. The stranger.

The homeless, get aid now and many have places to live and they have medical help, some draw disability. There are still some out there hurting.

There are others, some you would never know, you have to listen with your heart.

The Bible says the righteous care for the poor. Care means many things. Listen, visit, respect their wisdom. Share a meal. I know they hurt, I've seen it and hear it. They might be in your family of live next door. God may have given them something they need to pass to the next generation. You never know, you might find your best friend.

My Mother before she died said many things that never heard her say before. I cherish them, she even taught me a song, I'd never heard her sing.

She did become like the least of these. I saw it.

Whenever I set out to help someone, they helped me more than I did them. No joke. I Thank God for His goodness. His design is beautiful. He is about LOVE!

If you think you don't have time, ask God. He'll show you, you do. Matter of fact you'll be able to whistle while you work. You'll be blessed. Can't out give God! You reap what you sew, better than. You know God, He owns time too!

My best friend from school was a nurse, she came from a beautiful Christian family. Her father was a Minister, she was murdered at work. While she was working. Her ex-husband, came to the hospital, she was a nurse, with a gun and took her life.

It was so hard on her family. She had two little boys. Her mother was a beautiful lady, it was terrible what happened. Her Father, was so forgiving he preached her funeral and he, spoke of the forgiveness, he was able to find.

I went through severe depression, it was terrible. I hardly could function. She had just stayed with me in Texas. We had so much fun.

We always both loved God and would comfort one another with His word. It was horrible when I received the call from her family here in Indiana. My sweet, sweet friend. She had children. Her Mom and Dad, brother and sister, it was so hard. The following day my uncle who was close to my age died, from heart attack, two funerals, back- to- back.

It is so hard to lose those we love. God understands all our pain and it is painful for everyone.

I, returned to Texas, no family, depression set in, came back to Indiana rented a house. My Mom, introduced me to a lady who lived next to us and we grew a beautiful friendship. Approximately 3 years later she, became very ill, and was told she had 6 months, pancreatic cancer. It was hard. She added to who I was in Christ. Her husband also became ill and died shortly after her. I loved them. My husband would take him for his cancer treatments. They were so beautiful in Christ. They were poor and so giving.

We have to pay attention, this life no matter how long you live is short. Try to make the most of it.

Chapter 6

Bible says give and you will receive and that is true.

God has blessed my life with so many amazing and beautiful people. Thank You Lord for all you have done. I love you. I need you.

Having known all these people, I know I have indeed been rich. The spiritual blessings that were gained knowing those we love and spent time with.

Spir.it.u.al

adjective

1. Relating to or affecting human spirit or soul as opposed to material or physical things.

The Bible Study Downtown also would have a few little children. The home where we met belong to a young couple who did Foster Care. The babies made everything sweeter. Mom and I loved them there were two one would sit in her lap and one in mine. They were beautiful!

The Bible knowledge that some of the Homeless had was amazing I wouldn't want to leave. I Loved it.

Three of the homeless men did Street Preaching. One college student who was homeless was like sitting with one of the apostles. Another named Todd, was like a Prophet. One of the college students was baptized into Christ, given new life through Christ.

They would all help wash dishes and we would worship the Lord, while we worked. There were lots of dishes. The best helper was handicap and she always wanted to help. There were not many girls, it helped them to be with Mom and I. Mom and I loved it. Takes my breath away...love it! GOD IS IN SERVICE IT'S RELATED TO LOVE.

One gal could write poetry and another was missionary for the homeless, she moved in with a homeless man and lived on the streets. She needed me to help her, ask if I would. She went back home to her family and got off the street.

At the time we were going out regularly, there were several Christian Outreaches. The Government pretty much took over. Things changed a lot. It wasn't the same.

I cooked twice a week for Bible Study and twice a week for camps and streets. We fed 50 -200 each time.

Have you seen Jesus my Lord. You can see him in your own life if you look for Him.

We still go but most have housing now and it's different. They call us sometimes with a need and we take it to them, and we feed the few that's there still waiting on housing, occasionally.

It can be rough downtown and dangerous. We had problems at times, but God was with us.

O' He is the Rabboni. We love Him.

The preacher who taught the Bible Study had a nice family. His son helped a lot everybody loved him, so down to earth. Just comfortable to be around. Beautiful family.

One young man would have me bring extra sweet tea so he could drink it at his camp. He was the college student.

Another would text and say what's for lunch, he loved my spaghetti. I didn't have children that were my own and ended up with a bunch. I love it!

We did this many years.

I heard and read the Bible more downtown than anyplace else. I love God's word.

My cousin would go with me when Mom couldn't. She was a beautiful person, she loved them and she loved Jesus. She would always try to give me something for them. She passed away.

For several weeks I found myself just serving along with the others, and taking in what was being presented by the Lord. The most beautiful lessons for my soul. I was simply caught up in it the LORD! How he was demonstrating His self through all our lives, His love, His Body, and Service. Takes my breath.

The Lord became even more beautiful to me. Not only was we serving the poor, but they were serving us in other ways. I was listening and learning from them, together love abound, and all because of Jesus! Jesus is still serving all of us, even till this day.

Remember the song: JOY, JOY this is what it means: Jesus first yourself last and others in between.

LET NO DEBT REMAIN OUTSTANDING, EXCEPT THE CONTINUING DEBT TO LOVE ONE ANOTHER, FOR WHOEVER LOVES OTHERS HAS FULFILLED THE LAW.

ROMANS 13:8 ESV

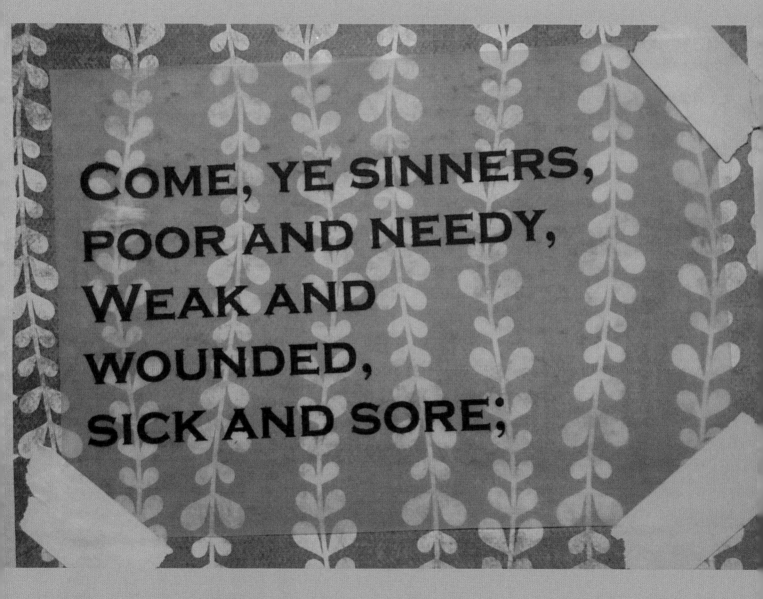

COME, YE SINNERS,
POOR AND NEEDY,
WEAK AND
WOUNDED,
SICK AND SORE;

Chapter 7

I sit up late, or get up early and pray for all the people we had in Bible Study, the poor, the oppressed, the suffering, and often times really sick.

My husband and I began to do street ministry 2009 – present. We learned their names we knew that this was important to God and needed also to be important to us. I found myself hurting right along with them. It felt like I was their mother. I liked that feeling. Who wouldn't? They need love, hugs, bandages, underwear and socks. I now had the attitude don't you dare hurt one of these. I just simply knew the Good Lord gave me a job to do. Thank You Jesus, I love You!

Listen: A CRUMB SHARED IS BETTER THAN A BANQUET ALONE.

Come, ye sinners, poor and needy, weak and wounded, sick and sore.

BE KNOWN TO US LORD JESUS, IN THE BREAKING OF THE BREAD.

All they asked was that We should continue to remember the poor, The very thing I was eager to do. – Galatians 2:10 NIV

Even the sparrow finds a home, and the swallow builds her nest for herself, where she may have her young –a place near Your alter, LORD Almighty, my King and my God. – Psalm 84:3 NIV

3 Praise be to the God and Father of our Lord Jesus Christ! In his great mercy he has given us new birth into a living hope through the resurrection of Jesus Christ from the

dead, 4 and into an inheritance that can never perish, spoil or fade. This inheritance is kept in heaven for you.

1 Peter 1:3-4 NIV

"In everything I showed you that by working hard in this manner you must help the weak of the Lord Jesus, that He Himself said,

"It is more Blessed to Give than to receive."

Acts 20:35 NIV

John (Chapter 13 A New Commandment) NIV

34 "A new commandment. I give to you, that you Love one another, as I have loved you also love one another. 35 "By this all will know that you are My disciples, if you have love for one another."

JOY OF THE REDEEMED

THE DESERT AND THE PARCHED LAND WILL BE GLAD; THE WILDERNESS WILL REJOICE AND BLOSSOM. LIKE THE CROCUS, IT WILL BURST INTO BLOOM;

IT WILL REJOICE GREATLY AND SHOUT FOR JOY.

THE GLORY OF LEBANON WILL BE GIVEN TO IT, THE SPLENDOR OF CARMEL AND SHARON;

THEY WILL SEE THE GLORY OF THE LORD, THE SPLENDOR OF OUR GOD.

STRENGTHEN THE FEEBLE HANDS, STEADY THE KNEES THAT GIVE WAY; SAY TO THOSE WITH

FEARFUL HEARTS, "BE STRONG, DO NOT FEAR; YOUR GOD WILL COME,

HE WILL COME WITH VENGEANCE; WITH DIVINE RETRIBUTION HE WILL COME TO SAVE YOU." THEN WILL THE EYES OF THE BLIND BE OPENED AND THE EARS OF THE DEAF UNSTOPPED. THEN WILL THE LAME LEAP LIKE DEER, AND THE MUTE TONGUE SHOUT FOR JOY.

WATER WILL GUSH FORTH IN THE WILDERNESS AND STREAMS IN THE DESERT. -ISAIAH 35:1-6 NIV

LOVE

We live sacrificially not because we feel guilty, but because we have been loved greatly. Now we find satisfaction in sacrificial love for others...by the way this is love.

We live in a world that thinks you just have to say I love you. I love everybody. It's not that easy: The Lord showed us what: LOVE LOOKED LIKE.

We have got to get busy. Work/Service/Action, are involved. There are many who are shunned by society because of sin (sometimes). Mental Illness or any other illness, their looks, their position in life (POOR), maybe they talk too much, maybe weight, over or under, old or some might think ugly, not as smart as we believe we are, their lack of education. Maybe they talk funny. The very ones Jesus seen and had compassion on. Most became His followers, Bible said uneducated where did all this knowledge come from people asked. They knew who these followers had been spending time with.

The very ones we might dismiss. Little upside down wouldn't you think?

EVANGELIST! REMEMBER THEM? THEY WENT BACK TO THEIR PEOPLE PROCLAIMING HIM TO BE THE CHRIST! The Bible says: and many believed!

Sacrificial love is not just our duty but our delight.

When I lived in Texas, before my friend, I mention earlier had died. I had made a friend out of someone who was seriously ill, to the point of death. He was a beautiful person he helped me with my depression from losing my friend. He and I would do meals on wheels together. He rode with me he knew all the streets. I picked him up every Sunday for Church and Wednesdays we did Meals on Wheels. He stayed active and went to Church every Sunday. His love for others was so sweet and sacrificial. He lived in a shed, before tiny houses were popular.

He kept to himself but had some words of wisdom. How blessed I have been. I wasn't going to mention that the above person had Aids, my husband thought I should include that information. You see we do all need each other. We all suffer at times. We need to carry one another's burdens the Bible says. Love one another.

We went to a small church maybe 50 people and the minister, his sermons each week helped me with the depression I, was going through. Right scriptures/words at the right time. Jesus caring for me through our minister and the Lord's words.

It was so hard losing my best friend to murder. Shot in the head. At the hospital where she worked. Beautiful family.

How beautiful is our Lord to care for each of us this much, you just got to catch your breath. GOD IS GOOD.

Another beautiful story which involves a sea of people serving and loving. There is a man that goes to church with us, who served in Vietnam, he suffers with schizophrenia, he loves to hang out all day in a shopping area on our side of town. You would not believe the people who know him and help him.

Young single moms who wait tables in the area restaurants. One told me she bought his lunch regularly. God has made all of us in His Image and this young gal has it going.

People, many different people buy him Starbucks cards, he loves them. He also loves Jesus and it shows, you would love him.

One day when I was gardening for a lady I work for, she started talking about him, cool everybody knows him and for the most part they love him.

Sometimes when you witness things like this you just want to sit at Jesus feet and stay there it's beautiful to see.

Today I stopped to get a fountain drink and I met two young men in line, both 23 and they took their time just to visit with me. I found out they did the same type of work as my husband and I. It cheered my heart.

Last night a lady was walking pass my house and she took time to speak with me. She said I love your gardens and I always walk pass to see them and tonight I wanted to speak and meet you. She had never seen me close enough to the street working. Today got to visit, we could talk. Beautiful person a police officer, both her and her husband. I am so thankful that they find joy in my gardens. I want others to enjoy them, take some flowers or some vegetables home with them.

Love and kindness are God's gifts we give to each other. Fruit of the Spirit. We just have to pick it!

Chapter 8

I have to admit it does seem like people all around are doing better, when it comes to finances, it's amazing. Everybody is on vacation and seem to be having a lot of fun, prettier, younger and healthy. I'm guessing most are doing good!

The Bible says the poor will always be with you. There's still poor, it's not just money people lack that makes one poor.

We just need to reach out more in our own families. With our family at church, we don't stop needing one another. Sometimes it's a stranger sometimes your mother, your sister, your brother, might even be the Lord.

Hey it's a fast track. Time maybe short.

It's beautiful when the body can come together and work as one. All parts necessary, even the least desirable.

So then neither is he that planteth anything, neither he that watereth; but God that giveth the increase.

1 Corinthians 3:7 KJV

I, pray if you're reading this you are encouraged, and know you are loved. Jesus, cares for each of us.

1 O give thanks unto the LORD, for he is good: for his mercy

endureth forever.

2 Let the redeemed of the LORD say so, whom he hath redeemed from the hand of the enemy: 3 And gathered them out of the lands, from the east, and the west, from the north, and from the south. -Psalm 107:1-3 KJV

GARDEN

Our garden is coming to a close, I have replanted a winter crop. Greens, lettuce, and cabbage.

I think vegetables are beautiful, love wheat fields, they are harvesting the beans and corn all around me, the beauty of those fields. I appreciate the farmers. When the snow falls, I'll build snowmen. Then spring YAY the garden!

"While the earth remains, Seedtime and harvest, Cold and heat, Winter and Summer, and day and night shall not cease." (sign of my porch taken from Genesis)

"For as the rain comes down, and the snow from heaven, And do not return there, But water the earth, And make it bring forth and bud, That it may give seed to the sower and bread to the eater, So shall My word be that goes forth from My mouth; It shall not return to Me void, But it shall accomplish what I please, And it shall prosper in the thing for which I sent it.

-Isaiah 55:10-11 KJV

Again:

So then neither is he that planteth anything, neither he that watereth but God that giveth the increase. 1 Corinthians 3:7 KJV

And he said, so is the kingdom of God, as if a man should cast seed into the ground; and should sleep and rise night and day, and the seed should spring and grow up, he knoweth not how. For the earth bringeth forth fruit of herself; first the blade, then the ear, after that the full corn in the ear. But when the fruit is brought forth, immediately he putteth in the sickle, because the harvest is come.

Mark 4:26-29 KJV

"The grass withers and the flowers fall, but the word of our God endures forever.

Isaiah 40:8 NIV

"O Lord, how manifold are all your works! In creation, in wisdom, you've made them all. Psalm 104:24 NKJV

The life of mortals is like grass, they flourish like a flower of the field; the wind blows over it and it is gone, and its place remembers it no more. Psalm 103:15-16 NIV

Chapter 9

Matthew 6:9-13 KJV

9 Our Father which art in heaven, Hallowed be thy name.

10 Thy kingdom come, Thy will be done in earth, as it is in heaven.

11 Give us this day our daily bread.

12 And forgive us our debts, as we forgive our debtors.

13 And lead us not into temptation, but deliver us from evil:

For thine is the kingdom, and the power, and the glory, forever.

Amen.

I pray that our best adornment is that of Jesus Christ, our glitter/sparkle is from His Light. Wrinkles: a map that leads to Him. In Jesus Name

Jump back or get back world, old age can look beautiful. The prettiest woman I ever seen was in Arkansas, at a restaurant. Her face resembled a map, seemed everyone in the restaurant, knew her. She had babysat most of them as they were growing up. I was young, she left a lasting impression on me.

She was neat made you think, as you heard their greetings towards one another. She was like a good book. She was cherished and loved.

I WOULD STOP AT THIS RESTAURANT FOR SOME SOUTHERN FRIED CATFISH AND SOME YUMMY HUSHPUPPIES, AS I HEADED TO VISIT MY FAMILY. I LIVED IN TEXAS. I WAS HEADED HOME TO SEE MY MAMA.

No Anti-aging treatment cures a heart and that reflects on a person's face. This woman had a heart and her face was like a bright light, she was beautiful. I have never forgot her these past 32 years. Christ was alive in her.

The Bible reminds us that outward beauty fades away.

I think: GRANDMA, could I have a cookie...sounds pretty good.

Try not to get caught up in a trap. Time to be wise the Bible says.

If you want/need Anti-aging - do your thing. If you are poor and can't afford it, well you're still beautiful. Learning to be content the Bible says is a good thing.

BLESSED IS HE THAT CONSIDERETH THE POOR, THE LORD WILL DELIVER HIM IN TIME OF TROUBLE. THE LORD WILL PRESERVE HIM, AND KEEP HIM ALIVE AND HE SHALL BE BLESSED UPON THE EARTH AND THOU WILT NOT DELIVER HIM UNTO THE WILL OF HIS ENEMIES. PSALM 41:1-2 KJV

CAST THY BREAD UPON THE WATERS FOR THOU SHALT FIND IT AFTER MANY DAYS.

ECCLESIASTES 11:1 KJV

THE LORD IS GOOD TO ALL; HE HAS COMPASSION ON ALL HE HAS MADE. PSALM 145:9 NIV

"Go ye into all the world, and preach the gospel to every creature". Mark 16:15 NIV

"IN THE WORLD YE SHALL HAVE TRIBULATION: BUT BE OF GOOD CHEER; I HAVE OVERCOME THE WORLD" JOHN 16:33 KJV

MANY ARE THE AFFLICTIONS OF THE RIGHTEOUS; BUT THE LORD DELIVERETH HIM OUT OF THEM ALL. PSALM 34:19 KJV

"IN RETURNING AND REST SHALL YE BE SAVED; IN QUIETNESS AND IN CONFIDENCE SHALL BE YOUR STRENGTH." ISAIAH 30:15 KJV

But he knoweth the way that I take: when he hath tried me, I shall come forth as gold. Job 23:10 KJV

O suffering, weary one, look now to the Lord and receive His comfort. He expends much labor upon us so that we may become what He desires. His purpose is to make us like himself and to bring out in every believer the highest in fruitfulness and service. Joy!

Faith and suffering; it is God's way of doing things. God's way is through the fire. He perfects us.

When you pass through the waters, I will be with you; and through the rivers, they shall not overflow you. When you walk through the fire, you shall not be burned, nor shall the fame scorch you.

Isaiah 43:2 NKJV

I have always loved the above scriptures. They show us we are indeed His workmanship. He will bring us through this. No matter who you are Christ said we can say we're rich.

It is often hard but he scatters moments of joy, food for the hungry and water for the thirsty.

His comfort who can deny, He comes to us in those precious moments.

Thank You Lord, for loving us.

He has met me in some dark and lonely places and stayed and gave me His company for a while. I know he's bottled my tears those visible and most of all the ones that flowed from my heart.

He has often times had to carry, my pain; the load was way too heavy, for my weak frame. I've been spent, my cup fills empty. He's here now with me. I need Him.

Those precious moments when it's just us and God.

He picks us up, breaths into us again.

Carries us sometimes for a short while and sometimes a long while.

He nurses us (Father's us), maybe I don't know I only knew a mother. Fatherless.

But HE IS HERE. He is our Father

Thank You Lord.

He's a FATHER to the Fatherless!

Another moment I have held onto is this: A man approximately my age, we befriended at Church said, he had found his suit at the Goodwill store down the street. His suit, looked nice, from the pocket he pulled his emptied communion cups, he said I've been to church this many times. Melted my heart. He went on to say he had been tithing and God had given him extra income that week, he wanted to know what I thought. I said sounds just like God. (pure and simple).

I love this kind of encouragement. God is beautiful and He is kind! The eye of the Lord is on each of us. Like a shepherd.

One Sunday morning after Church I noticed a bicycle with a little trailer behind it. I mentioned it to my husband. We came home, ate and later took a nap. I woke up before my husband and began reading my Bible. He woke up and asked where I was, I said reading my Bible. I was so hungry for God's word. I felt the Lord's Spirit on my heart.

We returned to Church that evening and went to class. Across from me sat a man I didn't know. We all began talking around the room. Later, (my husband and I) found out, the bicycle I noticed that morning belong to the man sitting across from me tonight. He had been insulted Sunday morning, he said by the sermon. He was also feeling insulted and hurt again this night.

Before our Sunday night Bible Study began:

The Lord's Spirit flooded my soul. I started saying scriptures that he needed. Not knowing they pertained to his hurt. This was all before class began. I didn't know what he was feeling in his heart or the topic. God, knew and He, supplied what was needed. We all opened our Bibles, the place from a book they were studying. Behold the same words I had spoken were before our eyes written. The teacher said this room is on fire tonight. And it was! This is where we were studying tonight. Bible says not to worry He'll give us the words and He did.

The man had been an orphan, grew up in Canada and was preaching across American, his transportation was his bicycle, with a little trailer. Big sign on back that read

GOD LOVES YOU.

God doctored his wounds and he felt better. My husband asked if he could come to our house to spend the night. He said yes.

We stopped at McDonalds to eat. After we got home, we visited a while longer and all went to sleep. It was a beautiful peaceful night.

The prayer he said after he was hurt was, God soften my heart and help me forgive the hurt I felt at Church today. I liked what he prayed and I use that same prayer from day to day. It's easy to get angry. The reason he told us his prayer, was he was having trouble forgiving them (the Church). The body, His people and we do fall short. All of us need forgiveness, and a fresh step forward.

AND NOW ABIDETH FAITH, HOPE, CHARITY, THESE THREE, BUT THE GREASTEST OF THESE IS CHARITY.

1 CORINTHIANS 13:13 KJV

Chapter 10

"LOOKING AT HIS DISCIPLES, HE SAID: BLESSED ARE YOU WHO ARE POOR, FOR YOURS IS THE KINGDOM OF GOD. BLESSED ARE YOU WHO HUNGER NOW, FOR YOU WILL BE SATISFIED. BLESSED ARE YOU WHO WEEP NOW, FOR YOU WILL LAUGH.
LUKE 6:20-21 NIV

You know I am so blessed, because, we grew up poor, maybe still poor, the family I grew up in lived the same. Aunts, uncles, grandparents. We always had gardens, cornbread, milk, something. We could feed someone who was hungry.

Where there is LOVE. (a stomach is easy to fill), where there is love and compassion.

Good conversation and a piece of cornbread can indeed fill you up, it's the LOVE, that is felt and that satisfies a hungry soul.

My table is from Victoria, Texas, from a convent we study the Bible and share hillbilly meals around it, everything in Texas is big, it's a big Table. My garden is bigger. If you are hungry, we'll see what we can do.

MY GOD IS SO BIG, SO STRONG AND SO MIGHTY, THERE'S NOTHING MY GOD CAN NOT DO.

HAVE I MENTIONED LATELY THAT HE LOVES YOU!

FORGOT TO MENTION GOD HAS A BIG, BIG HOUSE AND IT HAS LOTS AND LOTS OF ROOMS.

When you go out to serve in Christ, where you are is HOLY, HOLY Ground, He is among His Servants. Made Holy! There is POWER, POWER, WONDER WORKING POWER, IN THE BLOOD OF THE LAMB.

YOU'LL BE AMAZED HOW EASY AND WONDERFUL IT IS. YOU'LL GET PERSECUTED AND INSULTED, THERE IS ALWAYS CRITICS; HOWEVER THEN COMES THE LORD'S COMFORT IT WILL SWEEP OVER YOU. HE WIPES OUR TEARS AWAY! He puts them in a bottle.

WHEN YOU SEE JESUS EVERYWHERE - YOU'RE GOING TO TALK, JUST CAN'T HELP IT, TAKES YOUR BREATH AWAY. READ ACTS 4:18 NIV

GOD TAKES CARE OF US.

THIRSTY SOUL THERE'S A FOUNTAIN FREE, TIS FOR YOU AND ME...WILL YOU COME.

WE REMEMBER BEFORE OUR GOD AND FATHER YOUR WORK PRODUCED BY FAITH, YOUR LABOR PROMPTED BY LOVE, AND YOUR ENDURANCE INSPIRED BY HOPE IN OUR LORD JESUS CHRIST.

1 THESSALONIONS 1:3 NIV

We had some wonderful helpers. The elderly served with the greatest of care in everything they did, great detail and preciseness.

The very young with such enthusiasm. One young man Nathan, he served as an adult alongside me dipping plates. Once he was late and someone was doing his job. He was so disappointed, that was his job, he said. He loved when I would make biscuits and gravy (take breakfast) out. His father was a truck driver, new to Church.

There was a 80 year old man from Church, Freddy, he would always come, to our house and visit, he was great encourager. Even told me how to catch this dog I wanted. Another couple, Bill and Betty, Bill was an evangelist in California, worked with gangs, encouraged me to read: The Cross and the Switchblade. I finished it right before our friend died. They were beautiful. Our best friend was Margaret 94 years old. She stood beside us through thick or thin. She was always telling me how to drive, I couldn't drive fast enough, she would tell me when to go at the stop sign. We loved her so much.

Mother and her two daughters. Wow! They were workers and lovers. They brought clothes and tomatoes (baskets full). My husband and I love them.

I want to tell you when you're anywhere serving and God is with you, you're on HOLY Ground. You want to take those shoes off. God is AMAZING!

You are not serving alone. He is PRESENT!

The old hymn says: AND WHERE HE IS, IS HOLY!

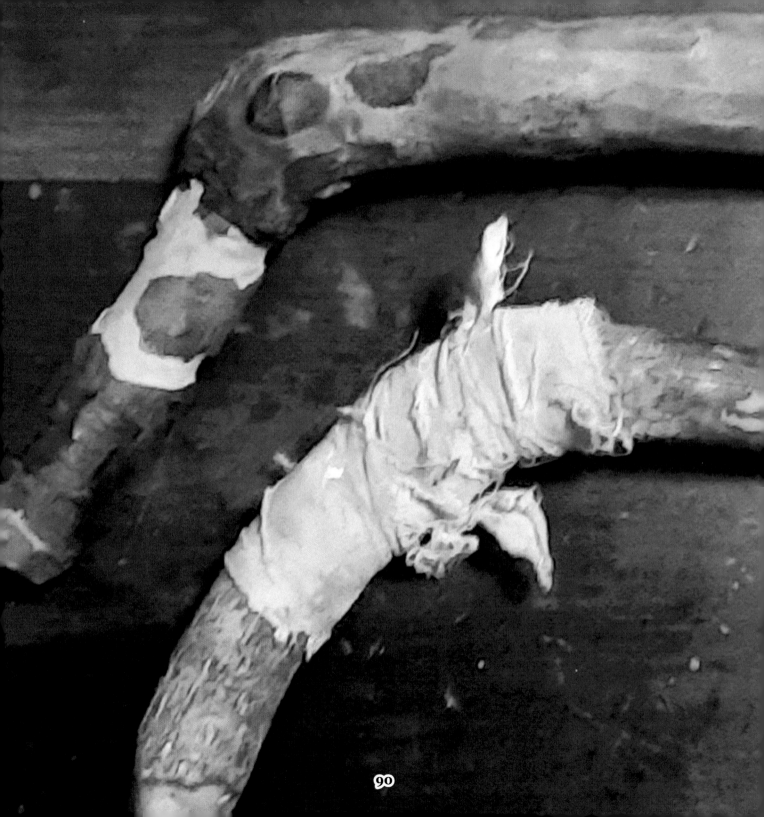

These warm my heart, primitive (early) homemade Garden tools. I am a gar.den.er

Just writing about Jesus.

Chapter 11

Where your heart is. We need to examine this question. Ask, the Father, to shine His light down upon us. Abundance is in Him, Security is in Him, Our Faith should be in Him.

It's not about everything we can get and spend. That is fun. It's not about that.

We know it's about giving and remembering others.

It's about true labor. Much is done in secret. Partly because it's became a part of you and you just do it, because it needs done.

That's not to stick you light under a basket. But someone needed you and the two of you bear witness to one another and God sees those things done in secret.

We do share, it can help encourage others. But you know these things.

Many pursue money and trips and just pleasure or fun. Later realizing that the fun, rest, or whatever we achieved from it, just simply didn't last. The things of God are Eternal, the joy and peace, and the

good loving thoughts, and loving memories, relationships go on. They continue and make for an abundant life. Blessing us and our family, our friends, the Lord's Church.

I have known a lot of poor people my whole life, they loved God and I looked up to them learned from them and knew without a doubt yep, they were in deed RICH!

I CAN'T HELP IT, HAD TO SAY THIS: WHO YOU LOOKING AT?

GOD IS GOOD, HE REMEMBERS ALL HE HAS CREATED. NOT JUST A FEW...ALL HE HAS CREATED.

WEAK MADE STRONG
POOR MADE RICH
HE SHOWS THE WORLD WHAT HE CAN DO.

Revelation 1:8 NIV

8 "I am the Alpha and the Omega," says the
Lord God, "who is, and who was, and who is
To come, the Almighty."

Psalm 138:1 KJV
Thanks to God from whom all blessings flow!!

FROM DUST

From the dust is who I am. I labor in prayer for my needs.

Every flower starts from a seed, a bud, and then it blooms.

(gar.den.er) Garden is what I do.

I want to be like a flower and one day BLOSSOM or BLOOM. More than that, I want to be serving where there's need. Maybe planting some seeds is what I'll do.

ksuhls

Song of Solomon 2:1-12 KJV
I am the rose of
Sharon, and the lily of
The valleys.

1. As the lily among
    Thorns, so is my love
    Among the daughters.

2. As the apple tree
    Among the trees of the
    Wood, so is my beloved
    Among the sons. I sat
    Down under his shadow
    With great delight, and
    His fruit was sweet to
    My taste.

3. He brought me to the
    Banqueting house, and
    His banner over me was
    Love.

4. Stay me with flagons,
    Comfort me with apples:
    For I am sick of love.

5. His left hand is under
    My head, and his right
    hand doth embrace me

I charge you, O ye
Daughters of Jerusalem,
By the roes, and by the
Hinds of the field, that ye
Stir not up, nor awake
My love, till he please.

6. The voice of my
Beloved! Behold, he
Cometh leaping upon
The mountains, skipping
Upon the hills.

7. My beloved is like a
Roe or a young hart:
Behold, he standeth
Behind our wall, he
Looketh forth at the
Windows, shewing
Himself through the
Lattice.

8. My beloved spake,
And said unto me, Rise
Up, my love, my fair one,
And come away.

9. For, lo, the winter is
Past, the rain is over and
Gone;

10. The flowers appear
    On the earth; the time of
    Singing of the birds is
    Come, and the voice of

    The turtle is heard in our
    Land;

Nature, gardening and farming. God chose to use these terms often.

REMEMBER JESUS ON THE SHORE FIXING BREAKFAST, HE INVITED HIS DISCIPLES TO DINE WITH HIM.

WE'VE ALL BEEN ASK TO DINE AT HIS TABLE. THE KING'S TABLE.

WE FEED UPON JESUS. WE ARE ALL LOVED.

As sorrowful, yet always rejoicing; as poor, yet making many rich; as having nothing, yet possessing everything. 2 Corinthians 6:10 NIV

In Christ we are complete. Take, eat and drink of Him.

Life from the fountain.

Poor in self and rich in Jesus.

The areas we grew up in were rough we have seen a lot of stuff. Our clothes mostly came from Goodwill, 3-4 large bags full at a time, Mom and us had no choice, it wasn't cool to shop at Goodwill, because you had no choice. We wore our shoes, until there were holes in them. It was rough. My Mom would maybe have .60 to last her until she got paid.

Mom would wash all the used pieces of clothing and polish all our shoes for church and school.

God was and still today is always Good. He has guided the way. I can smile and say Thank you Lord, for loving me and blessing me. It wasn't God who let us down. I'm so thankful I was taught to pray.

PEOPLE

Often times there have been those
That rubbed me the wrong way.
But then there were those who wiped
My tears away.
Ones who taught me the most
Valuable things and also
Those whos' presence could
Cause the scary ones to go away.
I even made a few friends along the way.
Jesus has loved me this way
He said they were treasure,
He will have stored for me that day.
The tools He chose to use.
He is the Potter; I am the clay.
ksuhls

Chapter 12

Let us lift up our heart with our hands unto God in the heavens. Lamentations 3:41 NIV

6 Then they cried out to the LORD in their trouble, and he delivered them from their distress.

7 He led them by a straight way to a city where they could settle.

8 Let them give thanks to the LORD for his unfailing love and his wonderful deeds for mankind,

9 for he satisfies the thirsty and fills the hungry with good things.

Psalm 107:6-9 NIV

Remember the hymn: Bread of Heaven feed till I want no more.

Don't worry for as long as the earth exist, there will be SEED TIME AND HARVEST.

You got me when I was an unformed youth, God, and taught me everything I know.

Now I'm telling the world your wonders; I'll keep at it until I'm old and gray. God, don't walk off and leave me until I get out the news of your strong right arm to

This world, news of your power to the world yet to come, Your famous and righteous ways, O God, you've done it all! Who is quite like you?

Psalm 71:17-19 MESSAGE

"What mighty praise, O God,
Belongs to you...
We will fulfill our
Vows to you, for
You answer our
Prayers. All of us
Must come to you.
Though we are
Overwhelmed by our sins, you
Forgive them all.
What joy for those
You choose to bring
near.

Psalm 65:1-4 NLT

"Remember those in prison, as if you

Were there yourself. Remember also those being mistreated, as if you felt their pain in your own bodies"

Hebrews 13:3 NLT

TRY to never leave someone to have to suffer alone. If they are locked in a prison, a nursing home, their own home, or in a state of mental illness (mental hospital). Lift them up in prayer, visit them, talk about things you know that they did in the image of Christ. Remind them how much they are loved Christ loves us. When we lose our freedom, it becomes a prison.

God made them everyone. For the most part they want to resemble their maker. CARE.

Most people are afraid and they don't really want to be alone or die alone. Someone might be crying for you today.

The poor and not just the poor, OPPRESSION, IS A FORM OF PRISON. There will always be someone who is pushed away. There will always be someone prettier and richer. God loves all of us.

Hold to God's unchanging hand, build your hopes on thing eternal, hold His hand.

Ask the Lord, to show you His beauty, look at the sky, pick some of his flowers, it's fall,

harvest time, the fields, the tractors and Our Farmers. I've always loved pumpkins of

every kind. Pick a pumpkin. Just soak in the Savior's LOVE! It has a way to brightening our faces.

GOD'S BEAUTY IS EVERYWHERE.

Chapter 13

The best company and the best friendship I ever had are with those that had no money, they were valuable, believe me. When God placed them in relationship with me, I grew more in Him. What a gift!

I learned LOVE, I seen how to have fun picking green beans, canning beans. Cleaning house, Getting a good cup of coffee from White Castle. Even pulling their weeds.

We would sing songs worshiping God and pray and read the Bible. We would share a meal at Ponderosa. Sometimes go to a Church Concert Worship Music downtown, Indianapolis. Sometimes we just folded laundry or cleaned house.

Ephesians 5:19-21 NIV

19 Speaking to one another with psalms, hymns, and songs from the Spirit. Sing and make music from your heart to the Lord. 20 always giving thanks to God the Father for everything, in the name of our Lord Jesus Christ. 21 Submit to one another out of reverence for Christ.

"Let the word of Christ dwell in you richly; teach and admonish one another in all wisdom; and with gratitude in your hearts sing psalms, hymns, and spiritual songs to God. And whatever you do, in word or deed, do everything in the name of the Lord Jesus, giving thanks to God the Father through him." Colossians 3:16-17 NIV

One of my neighbors down the street, a good time for us, was an evening in her living room drinking coffee and talking about Jesus. She like me loved the garden and we would talk about flowers and vegetables. She was a tiny lady, very quiet, I liked observing her, learning from her.

What Joy I had with these girls. What a gift of His Sweet Spirit!

This too was a bouquet of flowers from the MASTER. (bouquet of love, joy & peace). O the comfort of a friend that could celebrate and rest both In Jesus.

Amazing grace how sweet the sound.

Live a life filled with love.
Ephesians 5:2 NIV (read)

Growing up we were poor. We didn't know until people told us. Today, us kids laugh, we would tell Mom we were hungry and she would always say: if you're hungry eat an egg sandwich. My brother liked ketchup sandwiches. Our friends would be having pizza or a TV dinner, and even a pop. We were a family that was rich in Love. Love and Jesus – they go together!

You know I have chickens well I love a fried egg and biscuit sandwich. I love my chickens they all have names.

My school friends when I see them, laugh they remember me cooking for my brothers and sister and they say: you put everything you had in it and they would taste it and it was good. TASTE AND SEE THAT THE LORD IS GOOD!

Listen: NO TEARS IN HEAVEN

Heavenly Father, break our hearts so we see Thee, help us to love and have compassion for others as You want us to. You shared that LOVE IS WHAT YOU EXPECT from us; help us, Lord. To just simply LOVE YOU AND OTHERS ALL OTHERS in the way it is needed for each person.

You have told us over and over the value of each person their soul, and we should love them because we know - you do.

In Jesus Name Amen

Chapter 14

THE POOR/POVERTY/HIS PROVISION

Sometimes we have to speak up (be truthful)

To bring justice to a situation.

17 An honest witness tells the truth, but a false witness tells lies.

18 The words of the reckless pierce like swords, but the tongue of wise brings healing

Proverbs 12:17-18 NIV

This is one thing I believe in my heart: God is always good. He takes care of all of us, no matter how rich or poor we may be.

Jesus, was willing to make himself poor to save you and me. We are loved and God knows all about our joys, our tears, our hunger, and our needs and He promises to meet us there.

Blessed is he that considereth the poor: The LORD will deliver him in time of trouble. The LORD will preserve him, and keep him alive; and he shall be blessed upon the earth: And thou wilt not deliver him unto the will of his enemies.

Psalm 41:1-2 KJV

He That hath pity upon the poor lendeth unto the LORD; and that which he hath given will be pay him again.

Proverbs 19:17 KJV

He that despiseth his neighbour sinneth: but he that hath mercy on the poor, happy is he. Proverbs 14:21 KJV

HE HATH DISPERSED, HE HATH GIVEN TO THE POOR; HIS RIGHTIOUSNESS ENDURETH FOREVER; HIS HORN SHALL BE EXALTED WITH HONOUR. PSALM 112:9 KJV

He that giveth unto the poor shall not lack: but he that hideth his eyes shall have many a curse.

Proverbs 28:27 KJV

HE IS EVER MERCIFUL, AND LENDETH; AND HIS SEED IS BLESSED. PSALM 37:26 KJV

Charge them that are rich in this world, that they be not highminded, not trust in uncertain riches, but in the living God, who giveth us richly all things to enjoy; that they do good, that they be rich in good works, ready to distribute, willing to communicate;

(1 Timothy 6:17,18) KJV

And the Levite, (because he hath no part nor inheritance with thee), and the stranger, and the fatherless, and the widow, which are within thy gates, shall come, and shall eat and be satisfied; that the LORD THY GOD may bless thee in all the work of thine hand which thou doest. Deuteronomy 14:29 KJV

Rich in kindness, generosity, and thankfulness.

Always try to hold others in higher esteem than yourself.

Love your neighbor as yourself.

We must not get in the habit of trusting in false security, permitting the enemy to destroy who we are and our worth that is in the LORD.

It is so easy to give way to our wants and lust for more.

RICH IN FAITH AND OUR LORD.

We shouldn't grieve and oppose our loving Father who has and continues to care for all of us.

It's wise to study God's word as a family, to learn what it is to be obedient to our Heavenly Father. God does bless obedience. We all need His Blessings.

God is good, He is great whatever it is: He's got this.

Chapter 15

FOR HE SHALL DELIVER THE NEEDY WHEN HE CRIETH; THE POOR ALSO, AND HIM THAT HATH NO HELPER. HE SHALL SPARE THE POOR AND NEEDY, AND SHALL SAVE THE SOULS OF THE NEEDY. PSALM 72:12,13 KJV

YET SETTETH HE THE POOR ON HIGH FROM AFFLICTION, AND MAKETH HIM FAMILIES LIKE A FLOCK. PSALM 107:41 KJV

FOR THE LORD HEARETH THE POOR, AND DESPISETH NOT HIS PRISONERS.

PSALM 69:33 KJV

SING UNTO THE LORD, PRAISE YE THE LORD; FOR HE HATH DELIVERED THE SOUL OF THE POOR FROM THE HAND OF EVILDOERS. JEREMIAH 20:13 KJV

HE WILL REGARD THE PRAYER OF THE DESTITUTE, AND NOT DESPISE THEIR PRAYER. PSALM 102:17 KJV

HE RAISETH UP THE POOR OUT OF THE DUST, AND LIFTETH THE NEEDY OUT OF THE DUNGHILL PSALM 113:7 KJV

I WILL ABUNDANTLY BLESS HER PROVISION: I WILL SATISFY HER POOR WITH BREAD. PSALM 132:15 KJV

THOU, O GOD, HAST PREPARED OF THY GOODNESS FOR THE POOR.

PSALM 68:10 KJV

"LORD, YOU ARE MY STRENGTH AND FORTRESS, MY REFUGE IN THE DAY OF TROUBLE!" JEREMIAH 16:19 NLT

BUT MAY ALL WHO SEARCH FOR YOU BE FILLED WITH JOY AND GLADNESS IN YOU. MAY THOSE WHO LOVE YOUR SALVATION REPEATEDLY SHOUT, "GOD IS GREAT!" BUT AS FOR ME, I AM POOR AND NEEDY; PLEASE HURRY TO MY AID, O GOD. YOU ARE MY HELPER AND MY SAVIOR; O LORD, DO NOT DELAY.

PSALM 70:4-5 NLT

In the book of Job, Job speaks openly about his pain and grief to God.

God understands our pain and He knows our hearts. He wants us to talk to Him and to be honest and truthful. He cares.

2 For example, suppose someone comes into your meeting dressed in fancy clothes and expensive jewelry, and another comes in who is poor and dressed in dirty clothes. 3 If you give special attention and a good seat to the rich person, but you say to the poor one, "You can stand over there, or else sit on the floor" – well, 4 doesn't this discrimination show that your judgments are guided by evil motives? 5 Listen to me, dear brothers and sisters. Hasn't God chosen the poor in this world to be rich in faith? Aren't they the ones who will inherit the Kingdom he promised to those who love him? 6 But you dishonor the poor! Isn't it the rich who oppress you and drag you into court? James 2-6 NLT

I've been told there over 2,000 scriptures regarding the poor.

I mentioned earlier I was harvesting my potatoes and sweet potatoes, just finished my October beans (they're beautiful). I love gardening and I love my garden. I am sad to have to bring it to an end. I plan next years this winter. I wish you could see all the baskets of potatoes I have sitting in my dining room. (Faith like potatoes). God is Good!

But as for me, how good it is to be near God! Psalm 73:28 NLT

"Many are the afflictions of the righteous: but the Lord delivereth him out of them all" Psalm 34:19 KJV

Remember God's faithfulness. Read Psalm 44:1-3 and Psalm 34:19

Providence comes, there is Provision sent by God.

Make time to read God's word.

Pray (You can't grow without prayer).

Have faith and hope. Hope in God; for I shall yet praise him, who is the health of my countenance and my God". Read: Psalm 43:5 KJV

Read 1 Corinthians 13:12 NIV (seeing more clearly)

Take a look at John the Baptist and all the apostles and you'll note that it is not always roses and sunshine for those who follow Christ. We're told to pick up our cross daily.

Suffering has a way of making us humble.

The Lord has His way of helping the poor say I am rich. He blesses all He created. It's comforting, beautiful and true. Thank You Lord! The Lord provides.

We are told:

Your righteousness is as filthy rags in God's sight. "Not by works of righteousness which we have done, but according to his mercy he saved us." Read: Titus 3:5 KJV

In the Old Testament, when Israel was capture and taken to Babylon, the poor like farmers and gardeners were left to take care of the land.

Only the more desirable ones were taken into Babylon.

I love scripture that talks about planting and harvesting.

Jeremiah 4:3 NIV

This is what the LORD says to the people of Judah and Jerusalem:

"Break up your unplowed ground and do not sow among thorns.

(Uncultivated ground) could not produce fruit and grain. You have to work the ground or it becomes covered with weeds and thorns.

I also like:
John 12:24 ESV

Truly, Truly, I say to you, unless a grain of wheat falls into the earth and dies, it remains alone; but if it dies, it bears much fruit.

Now that I've grown older, I'll join the psalmist and say:

Even when I am old and gray, do not forsake me, my God, till I declare your power to the next generation, your mighty acts to all who are to come.

Psalm 71:18 NIV

When you feel tired take a rest. Tell the Lord what you are feeling, He understands. He truly loves us. Sometimes were hungry we need to eat, or read His word. Jesus, He is still here, washing our feet. He answers prayer, talk to Him about your needs. Thank Him for the things you know He did for you today.

There are times He leads us up the mountain where the air is fresh. Other times we're in the valley where there are pools of water and the green grass grows.

He takes care of us. He sees the sheep are fed. He's our Shepherd, He is faithful. If we need carried, He will pick us up. Trust in Him. He doesn't leave His flock, not one.

If God is for you who can be against.

Think about there is sweetness, there is a sunrise and then set, a rose garden, a bird sitting on its nest, sings best.

Can you see the Lord's hand, He takes care of us The Great I AM.

Again: I'll say: You are LOVED.

"God is our refuge

And strength, an

Ever-present

Help in trouble."

Psalm 46:1 KJV

Chapter 16

On bended knee we come,
With a humble heart we come,
Bowing down before your holy throne;
Lifting holy hands to you,
As we pledge our love anew,
We worship you in
Spirit,
We worship you in
Truth,
Make our lives a holy
Praise unto you,
Make our lives a holy
Praise unto you.

"Bow down thine ear, O LORD, hear

Me: for I am poor and needy."

Psalm 86:1 KJV

Father, please give us kinder; thoughts, words and actions. Maybe we all need these three. In Jesus Name Amen.

By his divine power, God has given us everything we need for living a godly life. We have received all of this by coming to know him, the one who called us to himself by means of his marvelous glory and excellence. 2 Peter 1:3 NLT

He who overcomes shall be clothed in white garments, and I will not blot out his name from the Book of Life; but I will confess his name before My Father and before His angels. Revelation 3:5 NKJV

5 For this very reason, make every effort to add to your faith goodness, and to goodness, knowledge; 6 and to knowledge, self-control; and to self-control, perseverance; and to perseverance, godliness; 7 and to godliness, mutual affection; and to mutual affection, *love*.

2 Peter 1:5-7 NIV

Saying it again:

Let no debt remain outstanding, except the continuing debt to love one another, for he who loves his fellowman has fulfilled the law.

Romans 13:8-10 NIV

2 Peter 1:8 NKJV

For if these things be in you, and abound, they make you that ye shall neither be barren nor unfruitful in the knowledge of our Lord Jesus Christ.

Please remember that it is wonderful if God has blessed you with everything nice.

For others who may appear to have less or not as nice as yours. God is still good to all of us and the truth is; if you are in Christ, you are rich in Him. We are all blessed in different ways.

Our race is in Christ, we all want to finish well.

True joy is in Christ and we all know our strength is found there.

For God so loved the world. All of us rich or poor are loved. We have a calling and we have all been equipped. We live blessed.

May God continue to Bless us and make us a Blessing to others.

Father God, please take care of our hearts, make them pure. Help us all continue to grow in LOVE. Love for You and for all others.

Help us to be beautiful in Your sight.

In our Savior's Name Amen.

Lord, us, our nation, our families help us not abandon You. We know You do not abandon us. Turn our hearts towards You. Help us seek You daily. We know You provide for us. We ask for our daily bread.

You are great and You meet our needs. Help us to celebrate with joy Your Greatness.

In Jesus Name Amen.

Chapter 17

5 He decreed statutes for Jacob
and established the law in Israel,
which he commanded our ancestors
to teach their children,
6 so the next generation would
know them,
even the children yet to be born,
and they in turn would tell their
children.
7 Then they would put their trust in
God and would not forget his deeds
but would keep his commands.
Psalm 78:5-7 NIV

You are beautiful, yeah
You are beautiful beyond description
Too marvelous for words
Too wonderful for comprehension
Like nothing ever seen or heard
Who can grasp Your infinite wisdom?
Who can fathom the depth of Your love?
You are beautiful beyond description
Majesty, enthroned above
And I stand, I stand in awe of You
Holy God, to whom all praise is due
I stand in awe of You
You are beautiful beyond description
Yet God crushed You for my sin
In agony and deep affliction
Cut off that I might enter in
Who can grasp such tender compassion?
Who can fathom this mercy so free?
You are beautiful beyond description
Lamb of God who died for me
And I stand, I stand in awe of You

I stand, I stand in awe of You
Holy God, to whom all praise is due
I stand in awe of You, O God

I stand and I will
I stand, I stand in awe of You
I stand, I stand in awe of You (holy God)
Holy God, to whom all praise is due
I stand in awe of You
Holy God, to whom all praise is due (holy God)
I stand in awe of You (awe of You)

You too are beautiful.

A time to shout with *joy* to the LORD God.

May each of us be encouraged, and encouragers, in CHRIST JESUS.

The Lord said, let the poor say I am rich. You are when you give your life to Christ, He's in you. You can do all things in Christ who strengthens you. Image the true treasure that is in you. The King, He's always with you. Jesus you are all world to us. Thank you, Lord.

Our Father in Heaven, help each of us be who You created us to be. Help us to put our faith in You to work. *You supply all that is needed,* let us:

Trust you and get busy loving You and each other and serving one another.

Thank You Lord for showing us what love looks like in the flesh. Beautiful beyond description.

In Jesus Name Amen

"ALL THEY ASKED WAS THAT WE SHOULD CONTINUE TO REMEMBER THE POOR, THE VERY THING I HAD BEEN EAGER TO DO ALL ALONG" "SHARE WITH GOD'S PEOPLE WHO ARE IN NEED. GALATIANS 2:10 NIV

I pray you know how deeply you are loved and that you would be encouraged. He has a plan for each of us.

For I know the plans I have for you," declares the Lord, "plans to prosper you and not harm you, plans to give you hope and a future.

Amen. Jeremiah 29:11 NIV

HARVEST TIME – SOME GOOD EATING. TALL GLASS OF ICE SWEET TEA AND SOME CORNBREAD THATS DRIPPING WITH BUTTER.

TASTE AND SEE THE LORD IS GOOD! BLESSED WE ARE WHEN WE TRUST IN HIM.

Before I close, I want to say to you that to lean into God, Our Father. God comforts us. I know life can be tough, it has been for me. Life is also beautiful. I realize when I recall His faithfulness, He has always held my hand. He is the great IAM. He cares for each of us, He knows our names and our troubles and He has a plan for you.

I love to shout and sing His praises and even dance, all because I know He loves me and I know He blesses me, sometimes it's the tiniest little thing. Sometimes it's big surprises like when it is dry and hot and we need rain. We all sometimes need rain. You see we all were poor. There was a debt. He came and lived among us. He served, He healed, He gave, He Hurt, He Died. He paid our debt, that we could not pay.

We have been provided - we were poor and in debt, He paid for you and me.

Talk with God about everything, every worry. He knows your name and He, cares for you and all your needs.

Prayers.

Not that I was ever in need, for I have learned how to be content with whatever I have. I know how to live on almost nothing or with everything. I have learned the secret of living in every situation, whether it is with a full stomach or empty, with plenty or little.

-Philippians 4:11-13 NLT

My stepfather, he would love to say: Remember when we were poor and so happy.

Both my stepfather and my Mom have passed I miss them, they were happy.

Remarks people sometimes make about you being poor hurts, especially when you're young. When you get older you remember the good things, like my Mom saving to take us kids to Kings Island. Oh how much fun we had. She was a good Mama.

I included a picture of her shortly before she passed. She had Dementia. She loved the Mardi Gras mask. She wore it everywhere I took her that day. I love her.

"I lie awake
Thinking of you,
Meditating on you
Through the night.
Because you are
My helper, I sing
For joy in the
Shadow of your
Wings. I cling to you;
Your strong right
Hand holds me
Securely.
Psalm 63:6-8 NLT

5 Your love, LORD,
Reaches to the heavens,
Your faithfulness
To the skies.
6 Your righteousness
Is like the highest
Mountains,
Your justice like
The great deep.
You, LORD,
Preserve both
People and animals.
7 How priceless is
Your unfailing love,
O God!
People take
Refuge in the
Shadow of your
Wings.

8 They feast on the
Abundance of Your
House;
You give them
Drink from your river
Of delights.
Psalm 36:5-8 NIV

I pray you find love, joy and comfort in the above scriptures. God reminds us over and over of His love and goodness to us all. He's so good!

Grace and peace be yours in abundance,

Kim

Printed in the United States
by Baker & Taylor Publisher Services